LIVING

HOW PLANTS BRING
THE EARTH TO LIFE

THE BLUE SKY PRESS

An Imprint of Scholastic Inc. • New York

SUNLIGHT

by **Molly Bang** &
Penny Chisholm

illustrated by **MOLLY BANG**

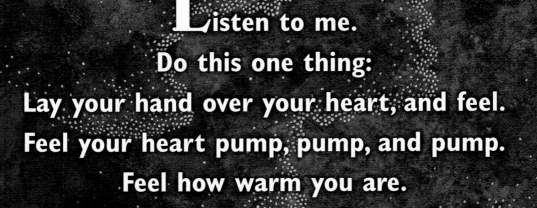

Listen to me.
Do this one thing:
Lay your hand over your heart, and feel.
Feel your heart pump, pump, and pump.
Feel how warm you are.

That is my light, alive inside of you.

I am your sun, your golden star.

I burn.

My light-energy explodes in all directions.

Most fades into endless space.

But some tiny, tiny part of my light
falls on your small planet
Earth.

I warm your land

and seas,

melt your glaciers,

create your winds.

I do all this.

But I do far, far more. . . .

My light becomes the energy
for all life on Earth.

All living things—
including YOU—
pulse with my light
and keep it circling
round and round on Earth.

How do living
things do this?

What is your secret?

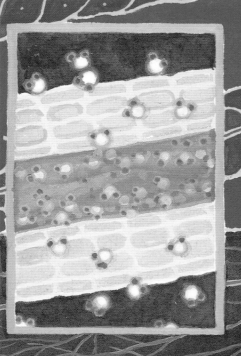

Your secret starts in plants—
green plants.

Plants suck up water—H_2O—from the Earth. In daylight,
green plants catch my energy with their chlorophyll.

Then . . .

KAZAP!

Plants use my energy to break apart the water—
break the H_2O into H and O_2, hydrogen and oxygen.

But as plants break apart the water,
they trap my energy as little packets.

Meanwhile, plants are breathing.
(Yes, plants breathe!)

They breathe out the oxygen
they broke off from the water
and breathe in
carbon dioxide—CO_2—
from the air.

Now plants use the packets of my energy
and the carbon dioxide from the air to build . . .
CHUNKA-CHUNKA-CHUNKA . . .

. . . sugar! And with this sugar, plants build all their parts. All the leaves and stems and juices, all the seeds and fruit and flowers of all the plants on Earth are built with sugar made from air and water using my light energy.

This is photosynthesis—
making life with sunlight, my light.

This is my gift of energy to you.

But wait! *You* are not green!

You have no leaves, no chlorophyll.

You cannot catch my light. And neither can your parents,
or your friends, your teachers,
or any reptile, insect, fish,
bird, or mammal in the
whole wide world.

So . . .

how do YOU get my energy?

Do you know?

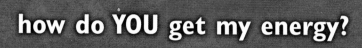

Yes, you eat plants. When you eat their leaves and stems and juices, when you eat their seeds and fruit and flowers, you eat my energy, my living light.

And plants do even more than give you food.

Remember how, in photosynthesis,
the green plants breathe out oxygen?

What happens to that oxygen?

It fills the air.

All the oxygen you living creatures breathe
comes from green plants.

Breathe in.

Feel the oxygen flow into your nose, your mouth—
all through your body.
Oxygen is a gift from plants to you. Your body uses oxygen
together with the sugars from the plants.
Your body burns them, slowly, to make the energy
you use to move and grow and live.

Without plants,
you would have no oxygen.

Without plants,
you would have no food.

Without plants,
you could not live.

Without plants,
there would be no life on Earth.

Now breathe out.

It is not oxygen that you exhale.

When you use the sugars from the plants for energy,
the sugars break apart inside your body,
changing back into water and carbon dioxide.

So now you breathe out carbon dioxide
and the plants all breathe it in.

They will use it to build more sugar—
food for themselves and other living things.

So you see?
Life keeps circling round
and round on your planet
Earth, through photosynthesis,
and through yourselves.

You share life with
everything alive.

Lay your hand over your heart and feel.

Feel my light inside of you.

You hold my light and make it live.

You are living sunlight.

NOTES ABOUT THIS BOOK

This is a book about life—about how life works. It is a book about how our sun gives us life through photosynthesis, the most important process on Earth. It is also a book about how photosynthesis connects all of life—how all life shares the same atoms, and how these atoms cycle on our planet.

WHY DID WE MAKE THIS BOOK?

Without photosynthesis our planet would be a lifeless ball of rock and water. Photosynthesis changes the "gas mass" of carbon dioxide (CO_2) in the air into the "solid mass" of plants—the plants that fuel all life on Earth. We made this book to help people understand this astounding phenomenon. We hope this understanding will help guide us toward a deeper sense of the unity of all of life.

SO HOW <u>DOES</u> LIFE WORK?

It all begins with the sun. Our star radiates heat and light in all directions, and a tiny part of that radiant energy hits Earth. But that tiny amount is still huge: The sunlight striking Earth <u>every eight seconds</u> equals all the energy from coal, oil, and gas we use in <u>one full day</u>.

   Most of this solar radiation weathers rocks, creates winds, controls the temperatures, and powers the water cycles of Earth. But a tiny amount of the sunlight hitting Earth is absorbed by plants and used in photosynthesis—and this makes all the difference. About 800 billion tons of plants are growing on our

Earth. Every year, through photosynthesis, these plants pull carbon dioxide gas from the air and build it into 60 billion tons of new plant tissue—new growth.

TREES AND ALL OTHER PLANTS ARE MADE FROM AIR???

Yes.

HOW DO PLANTS DO THIS?

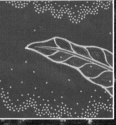

First, they use their green pigment, chlorophyll, to collect sunlight energy (in the form of photons, which are the little yellow dots that you see throughout the book). This process is illustrated in the insert where the chlorophyll "antenna" is shown

as a round-bellied green vase with many necks, down which the photon energy is being funneled to the "photosynthetic reaction center." Here, sunlight—solar energy—is converted to chemical energy; this is the factory that begins to make life from light.

   The special molecules produced in this microfactory are the "energy packets" in our story—the pinkish blobs that begin as rounded shapes but get "energized" with jagged yellow halos by the photon energy. These energy packets are central to the machinery of life.

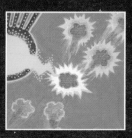

While sunlight is being collected by chlorophyll, the plant sucks up water molecules. These are shown as white balls (oxygen) with two blue balls (hydrogens) attached.

WHAT HAPPENS TO WATER IN PHOTOSYNTHESIS?

This is one of the most amazing parts of the process: Plants use the sun's energy to break apart water molecules and release hydrogen and oxygen. This is an extraordinary feat! If humans could figure out how to do this easily—split off hydrogen from water—we would have all the energy we need. This is the step in photosynthesis where oxygen gas (O_2) is made and released into the air. This is where all the oxygen in our atmosphere comes from. This is the oxygen we breathe, the oxygen that keeps us alive.

So far we have shown how plants convert the sun's energy into chemical energy—energy packets—and we have shown how they make oxygen, but . . .

HOW DO PLANTS CHANGE "GAS MASS" TO "PLANT MASS"?

As the plants are "breathing" out oxygen, they are also breathing in carbon dioxide from the air. They need to use the carbon dioxide in the final step of photosynthesis: making <u>sugar</u>. In the pictures, the double white balls in the air represent the oxygen molecules, and the double white balls with the black ball in the middle represent the carbon dioxide molecules.

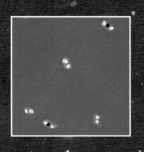

Chemical energy, carried in the energy packets, and carbon dioxide molecules both enter the huge orange ball. Inside this ball, the carbon molecules from carbon dioxide are joined together to make sugar molecules. In the picture, you see them fly out of the ball to the right.

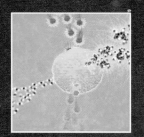

<u>SUGAR IS THE FINAL PRODUCT OF PHOTOSYNTHESIS.</u>

WHAT KIND OF SUGAR DO PLANTS MAKE?

This is not just any old sugar like the fine crystals in our sugar bowls or the corn syrup in soda pop. This is a particular kind of sugar called glucose ($C_6H_{12}O_6$). Glucose is "energy central" in life processes.

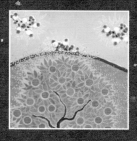

Notice that the energy packets, which are flying out the bottom of the orange ball, have lost their halos. Their energy, originally from the sun, has been transferred to the bonds that hold the sugar molecules together.

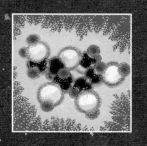

What does the huge orange ball in the picture represent? This is the enzyme called "Rubisco." (This is its nickname. Its real name is ribulose bisphosphate carboxylase.) Rubisco is the workhorse of photosynthesis, and it is part of an extraordinarily complex chemical pathway. Rubisco grabs carbon dioxide that has drifted in from the air and starts building it into sugar. Rubisco is <u>the</u> molecule that converts the "gas mass" to "plant mass" in photosynthesis. It is the most abundant, and arguably most important, enzyme on Earth.

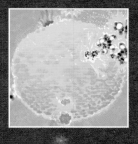

So, to sum up so far:

<u>Green plants use energy from the sun to make sugar from carbon dioxide and water, and at the same time, they release oxygen into the air.</u>

This is photosynthesis.

We can write this out as a chemical reaction:

CARBON DIOXIDE GAS (CO_2)
+ WATER (H_2O)
+ SOLAR ENERGY (PHOTONS)
react and make . . .
SUGAR ($C_6H_{12}O_6$)
+ OXYGEN GAS (O_2)

Once the sugar is made, plants can use the energy and the carbon in this sugar molecule to make all the other molecules in their bodies, and do all of the work they need to do to stay alive.

But plant sugars don't only fuel and become plants. All people and other living beings live by eating plants, or by eating another organism that has eaten plants, or by eating an organism that has eaten an organism that has eaten plants, and so on.

This "food chain" links the carbon of all life back to plants and photosynthesis and, most importantly, back to the sun.

But plants give you more than just food. Remember, oxygen is a <u>very important</u> by-product of photosynthesis! It created Earth's atmosphere as we know it. This is the oxygen we breathe. It sustains all animal life on Earth.

HOW DO WE GET ENERGY FROM THE PLANTS WE'VE EATEN?

We digest them, of course. But what does this really mean? In fact, we burn the plants, using the oxygen we breathe. Think of a wood fire. The fire requires oxygen to burn, and it gives off energy as heat. It also converts wood—"plant mass"—to carbon dioxide gas.

We have the equivalent of a wood fire inside our bodies, but it is a slow, low-temperature burning of our food. Our bodies consume oxygen, release carbon dioxide, and capture the energy from our food in the form of "energy packets" very similar to the ones produced in photosynthesis. These packets fuel all the chemical reactions of our living bodies.

To sum up again: People, and all other living beings, get the energy we need to live by using oxygen to break down sugar made by plants, and breathing out the carbon as carbon dioxide. We capture the energy released from the sugar as chemical energy—but now it is in the form of small "energy packets" that can be used for the multitude of things our bodies need to do to stay alive.

Sound familiar? It should. Because this process, which is technically called "respiration," is almost the exact mirror image of photosynthesis!

The chemical reaction for respiration is written as follows:

SUGAR ($C_6H_{12}O_6$) + OXYGEN GAS (O_2)
react and make . . .
CARBON DIOXIDE GAS (CO_2)
+ WATER (H_2O)
+ CHEMICAL "ENERGY PACKETS"

This is the <u>Cycle of Life</u>: Plants change "gas mass" to the "solid mass" of their plant bodies through photosynthesis, and then we eat the

plants and change the "solid mass" back to "gas mass" through respiration. Photosynthesis produces oxygen and consumes carbon dioxide, and respiration consumes oxygen and releases carbon dioxide. In the process, solar energy is converted to chemical energy—the energy of life. And so the cycle circles round.

Every second of every day, this Cycle of Life is revolving everywhere on Earth. Each year, billions of tons of carbon dioxide are drawn from the air by all the plants and trees on Earth and converted to plant mass. This total global photosynthesis is roughly balanced by the amount of total global respiration. This balance of production and consumption prevailed in Earth's recent history—say, the last 100 million years. It is this balance that helps maintain the amounts of carbon dioxide and oxygen in our atmosphere. What happens if the balance is suddenly disrupted? That's another book!

ADDITIONAL INFORMATION

Obviously, in this book we have had to simplify a <u>lot</u> of things. Painful as it was, we had to leave some critically important parts of Earth's machinery out of our story. Here are a few of the most important ones.

The first and most important omission is the <u>phytoplankton</u>, which just happen to be Penny's life's work. Phytoplankton are microscopic single-celled plants that inhabit all of the bodies of water on Earth— oceans, lakes, ponds, rivers, puddles, and even icebergs! They are everywhere, but they are invisible to us. There are <u>100,000</u> phytoplankton in a teaspoon of ocean water. Yet, even though the total weight of all the phytoplankton is only <u>1/1000</u> as much as all the trees and plants on land, phytoplankton perform roughly <u>half</u> of the Earth's global photosynthesis. They feed all the bacteria, zooplankton, fish, whales, and other creatures living in lakes and oceans. They are extraordinary in their diversity and versatility. But this, too, is another book:

Our second large omission is a group of bacteria that are descendants of the first life on Earth. They are a special kind of "photosynthetic bacteria" that live in water and mud that is devoid of molecular oxygen. In fact, oxygen is poisonous to them! These bacteria live in areas where there is abundant hydrogen sulfide (H_2S), the compound that makes swampy mud smell like rotten eggs. Like plants, they build sugar from carbon dioxide using solar energy, but they build it without making oxygen. During photosynthesis, these bacteria break apart hydrogen sulfide (rather than water) and release sulfur rather than oxygen. And there is even another kind of bacteria that can build sugar from carbon dioxide without using sunlight at all. They use "chemosynthesis" to do this, and they are called "chemotrophs" ("chemical eaters"). They can extract energy from compounds like hydrogen sulfide through chemical reactions, and they use the released energy to build sugar molecules from carbon dioxide. So when we say in the book: "Without plants there would be no life on Earth," this is not strictly true. Microbes inhabited Earth before plants evolved billions of years ago, and similar microbes live in environments where there is little or no oxygen today. These microbes were an important part of the history of life on Earth and are a small, but important part of the living world today. Microbes are the most versatile metabolic machines on the planet.

Finally, there are two oversimplifications in the book that need clarification. The first is when the sun says to humans, "You cannot catch my light." We actually <u>do</u> catch sunlight. This is how our bodies synthesize Vitamin D, for example. The point here is that we cannot catch sunlight, photosynthesize, and make our own food from the air.

The second oversimplification is when we say that living beings are built from carbon, hydrogen, and oxygen. They are. But there are other atoms that are also important parts of life's machinery, primarily nitrogen, phosphorus, sulfur, and iron. Many other elements—such as cobalt, chromium, copper, zinc, and selenium—are found in only tiny amounts in living beings but play vital roles in life's work as well. All these atoms cycle through life on our planet.

To Ben, who delighted in knowing that he is— and all of us are—dancing sunlight—M. B.

For Don, Jack, and Gus—P. C.

Our thanks to Jim: mediator, translator, and explicator, and without whom this book would not have been possible

THE BLUE SKY PRESS

Text copyright © 2009 by Molly Bang and Penny Chisholm
Illustrations copyright © 2009 by Molly Bang
All rights reserved.
No part of this publication may be reproduced, stored in a retrieval system, or transmitted in any form or by any means, electronic, mechanical, photocopying, recording, or otherwise, without written permission of the publisher. For information regarding permission, please write to: Permissions Department, Scholastic Inc., 557 Broadway, New York, New York 10012.
SCHOLASTIC, BLUE SKY PRESS, and associated logos are trademarks and/or registered trademarks of Scholastic Inc.
Library of Congress catalog card number: 2008014238
ISBN-13: 978-0-545-04422-6 / ISBN-10: 0-545-04422-7
19 18 17 16 15   19 20 21 22 23
Printed in China   38
This book was printed on paper containing 50% post-consumer waste recycled materials.
First printing, February 10, 2009
Designed by Kathleen Westray